Traces of Her

This book is a work of fiction. Names, characters, places and incidents are products of the authors' imagination or are used fictitiously. Any resemblance to actual events or locales or persons, living or dead, is entirely coincidental.
An Original Publication of Teryn Williams. ©2014 Teryn Williams.

Cover Art owned and created by Teryn Williams. ©2014 Teryn Williams.

All rights reserved. All works of art remain the sole right of the author. No parts of this book may be reproduced, stored in a retrieval system or transmitted in any form or by any means without the prior written permission of the publisher or author of artwork, except by a reviewer who may quote brief passages in a review to be printed in a newspaper, magazine or journal.

First printing August 2014

ISBN-13: 978-0692276266
PUBLISHED BY TERYN WILLIAMS.
Printed in the U.S.A.

*You taught me something
Something took me half my life to learn
When you give all yourself away
Just tell them to be careful of your heart*

-Tracy Chapman

Honesty (The Opening)

  We tip toe around love because it is so hard to outline. Everybody has their meaning of what and how it should be. They assume that their love is superlative, because she is busy loving you the way that she wants to be loved. And you, you are busy loving her the way you need it to be experienced. We see with our own hearts and not the desires of others. This is how love ends before it ever arises.
She is stuck in her own mind, battered and damaged from living too soon. She thinks that love is something that you give and cannot be reciprocated. The poor souls that she mates with never have a chance, it is a competition that they are not aware of. It is a battle against her estranged parents, much older first girlfriend and a stranger she trusted too much in.
  She creates relationships with fairy tale beginnings, never acknowledging the mud she will drag in behind her once she has you settled down. She is breathtaking with her intellect; it makes up for the beauty that she denies herself. Her lies are the only honest things that she possesses.
She loves out of commitment; her heart is not involved, too full of self-destruction. She is torn up by the affection she denies herself in the presence of her lover, because she is a self-professed philanthropist.
I saw her, giving self-passion in the dark, the same caresses she rejects from her lover. She claims to be a "touch me not," though she climbs all over herself and cries about her selfish lovers. A mother of her own pain, she licks it up like a last meal. She draws the ends of her relationships on her thighs, a self-declared soldier.
  Her name is mine and mine is hers and yours alike, we have all met her, loved and hated her the same. She is still ablaze, searching for love to love her back while taking prisoner her freedom to do so. A contradiction is what she is, what we are, when she, when we let her in instead of out. I'm trying to avoid her, with her attractive mind and well put together story, it sort of matches

mine. We compare notes, pros and cons and then compromise our hearts to not be lonely.
She is who we are. Do not allow her to stay, she is not honest.

Dedication: To Audre, and the courage to love without shame

Traces of Her

I was born on Doomsday
Chocolate oblivion
Eyes wider than permitted
God had shown Himself
Unrestricted

My mother was a child
Swelled ignorance
Colored in Emeralds
I came to be here
Veiled with her
Weakened Truth
I survived

In those awkward moments
I ached
For arms sturdier than pride
Wet like tears
I waited on Love
Naïve Solitary

My frame his doormat
My heart her switch
Dooms day
I birth
A wilted May Flower
I am

Root Woman

You loved me different
With your serpent tongue
Tattooed with lies
I enjoyed hearing

Your asinine lullaby
Full of lure
Laced with hoodoo

You with your hocus-pocus
Fire red smoked vocals
Proud to be living out loud
Beautiful and brown eyed
Lust filled devil

Me with my weak self
Spellbound and trapped
Alone in your now
Dilapidated house of a heart

Where my devotion
Is still attached
To fictitious promises
Conjured up by you
Root woman

Panama

Beneath the rain's face
I stand exposed
Washing locks of hair
Wondering if…
Your X'd Lovers
Would laugh my way
Knowing how I caress myself
Counting the times
We do not make Love
Our suppressed appetites
Are atrocious
In their sexed famished copy of you

What is it that you Love
About me
Lessened desires
How I slumber against your embraces
Obliviously you journey a headstone
As I trip over your past frequently

Is there a difference in history
Those I left behind
Not adequate
Do I sustain you

Please…no sham
The truth is enough

Are you well nourished
Lying by, but not with me.

It used to downpour
During our creation
Wild flowers bloomed with dew

Now wilted in this drought

Unvalued glimpses of hope
Mislaid in your reluctant mind
If only you knew...
If only I sought to illuminate
Above
My need to be unspoken
We could travel beyond
This disaster
To labor a new storm

Panama
I miss your tears

Audre,

Why is it that time does nothing to comfort my moods for you? You are motivation beneath my misery...wings to conquer my goals.

Trance

My dreams are white with veils
Angels for babies
Crying in my sleep

My visions are colors
Different than yours
Seashells lying at the shoreline
Fading and abandoned

I have fantasies of us
Dressing in the same name
Nude and shameless

Sometimes I run from here
In search of my own imaginings
Without the fear of losing you
I embrace all of me

As I reach for air
I should not breathe without
The life I desire to dream

And you my love
Should be free of my reveries

Sorry

Morning rises
We all descend
Below the sun
I am desperately crawling
Towards you

Secure me a way
To your mercy

This is my confession
I own the breaks in your heart

I have not spun from air
My probing soul
Searching your release

And if these words shall never reach you
The place I once pledged my loyalty
I must find another way
To bury the deceit I nourished you

My intentions were to honor our vows
My need to self serve was greater

It is my regret
When I must now shape words
To ease my remorse
To soothe your pain

Night bows
We all plunge
Beneath the moon

I am sorry

Still not a Poet,

I am not a poet; words flee me when I desire them the most. I am not a poet because my lovers won't love me the way I suffer it. I bear the distance emotions can crawl beneath the design of the heart and beat you to death. I am but a creation formed from leftover choices between right and wrong, an unconditional art of purgatory. I lie in between my dreams and what's destined for me. A struggle to position my lips with sentiments never comprehended beyond the core of a stripped soul. I am not a poet for satisfaction escapes me, when I want to embrace her less arms, she shall never feel my intentions carved with verses I wish to sing. I am not a poet for this bird is enslaved without a song.

Patience

In this last hour
I move only
To search your eyes
To awaken me
I molest your lips
Painted with guilt
Dry as truth
Against our vivid dreams

I need you
However probable
Old words
Faded images
Stolen glances
Of a voice
Still lingering in your verses
I heed you
Echoing

My Love
These ruins
You left behind
Should be sketched and hung
On the walls of your heart

I shift only
In these last hours
That I might stumble
Upon your splendor
Once again

Once I set you free
My truth will be known
And you will breathe

All the lies I feed you
To feed me
Have been so unfulfilling
If only the past could be returned
I would give you back your stuff
Return these eyes hungry with passion
To a starving girl

I released all too soon
My aspirations were more than you could handle

A coffin built to last

If only time would sit here
In this moment
If you would have me
I am available to you

Lock & Key

You entered me with your heart
I had a dagger in mine
The break was ordained

We conjured love from air, depending on heaven in the end. If only you had not ignored your truth throbbing below your need, you would have discerned my lack of presence.

I am sitting here now calculating your beliefs of me and offering up nothing. I am not your altar or anything that dreams.

I am spun from a web of disgrace openly, failing to please unpleasant things I give in greed. My desires are weights your arms alone are unable to embrace.

Release me to the night where I belong
Slumber me beneath the constellations
Where love is unmade into anything I aspire

You are not my destiny
I have yet to craft my own

You penetrated me with your soul
Wide eyes shut tight
I was born blind
Never will I see you
Again

Saving Grace

I want to love
Something I've never done before

Tied to a rope in prayer...ascending
My flesh in her hand
I am melting
Like a candle's last flame
She bows before me
To kiss her pain

I fell in love with the tracks she laid for me to travel in her wind.

We are both children of the earth destined to revolve before we explode into dust.

I christened her my lord
As she descends when I call
This is not love
I'm endorsing
Sharp ends for air

Traces of Her

There is no love between your legs. I just want the climax.

I Still Do

Because I need you to know:
I love you
In spite of myself

Not even your pain could erase the creation of us

We were unleveled
With you offering more than I would
I own that

And this is my confession:
I was untrue, you were right
Never doubt yourself again

But you are not the moderator of my heart
You will not testify on my behalf
Nor rephrase what I felt
I love you
You will always hold that

No amount of blame will change facts:
I failed us
Like a coward
I ran away from everything I ever wanted
You

And I cannot honor your wish
To rearrange my steps
To make that day disappear

When you said hello and swallowed my breath

"This arbitrary woman of a shell"

Traces of Her

Maybe that is easier for you
To dye my heart as blue as your veins

But if you ever want to be closer to my truth
Come upstairs
Where I am barefaced
In all my fuck-ups

I will express regret for everything
Except loving you

Remind Me

You may need these words one day
To remind me
How I once felt about us

In that moment
My lunacy will overshadow any logic
On my way out our door

Don't let me leave

Remind me how you are a lifelong need
Not some temporary desire
Tell me
How much I wanted this…us…you
Repeat it again…

How I will regret it
When I'm spinning on the opposite side of this evolution
Without…us

You won't be there
Wrapped around my waist
Inhaling my flesh
Snoring softly

Remind me that I will lose all of that

And how I will be afraid of the darkness
Once again
It's because of your existence
That I have light
In the curve of my heart
Where you beat
When you woke me from my slumber

Traces of Her

Remind me

Use these words that I gift you today
Hold me prisoner to my terms
For I am indebted
To your love

Please
Don't let me leave
Throw my words back my way
And remind me
How I still believe in us

Blue Mahoe,

I love you. It is the most tragic thing, because there is nothing I can do about it. The woman is someone you used to be and somebody I still strive to create within myself. Six years and time stands as sturdy as it will...against my own desires. I have settled for a healthy love of my own, reminisces of yesterday...us, we linger today.

Homemade Love

There is a love unmade between us
Something asymmetrical
Where I deserve unrestricted worship
At my troubled Temple

Where you require someone
Arched at your feet
In the contradicting poses you desire

Not a blind spot
Of constant forgiveness
We give under silent ultimatums

Truth is...
We swim in opposing oceans
A temperature of disconnection

Drowning whatever we were
To return a grave of memories
Once laced with charm
Is now fading with sentiments of treachery

"Pardon me for promising forever...it was never mine to give"

I chose love over wisdom
A fault I continue to carry

Southern Comfort

You were right
I am smoke
Burnt bitter sweet
Southern honey dripping
From a razors edge

But I did not hide these wounds
My love
You humped every scar I possess

Even when I set you free
You came again
Without invitation
To give ultimatums to ashes

What causes you to revisit
This grave
Something you swore to bury

While I am still biting
Bitterly
In your mouth
You should use your head
To find a way
To resist your mistakes
My love…

Expressions

I Am Poetry
Conveying my position
In tulips
In purple
In song
Stained pages of flames
From the grave of my mind
Words pour anxiously
For survival
Grasping
Beseeching
A necessity
To attach with mind-set
To sync with heartbeat

I Am Poetry
Once a girl, now a woman
Dilapidated
Hesitant and drifting aimlessly
In her make-believe world of words
That paints her reality
Of something celestial beyond the sky
Mystic beneath the ocean's floor
In moon dreams
Sun fantasies
And everything amid
Because my words embrace
When hands can't
When hearts won't
When people forget
Poetry will be there
With expressions of love
Verse of touch
Sympathetic prose

To embrace this fear
To cradle nightmares
A mask for fear
Poetry gives devotion
Eases hate
Persuades
Heartstrings to play songs
To calm unforgivable things

I Am Poetry
A body of words
Twisted in a river of tears
Beneath a fading sun
Creating rainbows to latch on

Sun Rise

Sunday mornings
Are dreary
As we dress up
Smiles
Kissed
With fictitious love

Is it worthy
This space
We create
To exist in doubles

Is it better than nothing

Swollen appetites
Occupied
With yesterday's memories
How air was free

Sunday morning
I'm lonely
She is here
Beside me
Wanting
The same thing

Fire
From History
Smothering this deathbed

We have settled
In ruins
We shall remain
Crypts of our past

Teacher,

It is the most freeing thing to just allow love to love without limitations. I am on a journey of exploration, of learning me and how to love and hurt and joy. My definitions of everything have been taught, time to unlearn those ties to this grave... I just want to live and taste lips and learn different languages of affection. I am not my lover and she is not me...I am my lovers and they are me. My desires are not one dimensional or tied to her heart break, Love is not pain...it flows naturally to where and whom it should be. I loved a girl last night and she loved me back...I twice loved on the same night, different girl and she comforted that need to spread all the love I had leftover from my marriage to another Lover that showed me how to be love..I am grateful for our beginning and her creation of me. She birthed me, carried me, taught me beautiful and all the things I should be to my next lover.

Misplaced Inspiration

Nothing draws her
Poetry
She once authored
Stained with tortured
Heartbeats

Now silenced
The dunce
Warmed by her
Hand for limb
Compassion
Stalled desire

Sundown
Corners black and wet
Barriers bare
With a faded smile
She traded
Pain for tedium

A shadow of self
Leftover
Passion failed
For gray acquaintance
I am here
She is around

I Really Want You

When we argue
My head aches
Words become foreign
The message lost
You cannot hear
What I'm really saying
I fear losing you

My heart beats
Louder than usual
The flames rise
We burn

Beneath the true reason
I really need you
Something unheard
When voices are crying

I can't live without you

Suppressed aside the anger
I shed in silence
These tears
Is the love
I have for you

Repentances

Thinking of you
In your space
Wondering
Where you drift to
When you go under

Desiring
Your fingers over mine

I should be there
Aside
When you awake

I woke this morning
With your hands
Cuddling my face
I smiled
Inside
Your comfort

My arms should be
Your embrace
When you recover

Love Stones

Onyx:
Beautiful cat eyed Negro
With a balled up fist
Smooth as the silky lies
She sold
A broken woman
Cracked in a wise way
She left me

Pyrite:
Gold
She was earth and fire
A lady's woman
Searching Jesus
She found her way
Home through me
I found mine

Carnelian:
She relaxed me
Freedom
She gave to me
My voice
Fed my hunger
She delivered me
My first real love

Ruby:
Because she was
Her mother's spawn
So much greed
She took what she gave
Leaving music
As the only proof

Traces of Her

That we existed

Snowflake Obsidian:
I was her first
Speck of color
She didn't notice
Til my hair curled up
Scared her to death
Full lips and all
I never really loved
Anything about that girl
Though I do now

Tigers-Eye:
Jamaican soiled
American borrowed
Love of my life
In a bottle
Is where I keep this heart
She gave me
Everything
Taking nothing
But my breath

Lace Agate:
She was hard
With frills beneath
Her tongue lied
On every heart
She denied
Her own self love
We shared
A bloody goodtime
Until the sun rose
On our demise

Moss Agate:
My warrior
My want
My need
My end

Before I give again
These Love Stones

Whisper

Her name is a whisper,
not my secret but hers. She is my lover,
amongst other things. She comforts the aches,
along with the troubles of my existence. I breathe
for the sole reason of love. Her love
is heavy, but vital. She has the feel
of a deity. I bow down to her,
day one. It was a salutation from hell,
her spirit tattooed on arm. I licked
before healing. She ate while full,
we were gluttons together. Starving
for what we had. Before us
was the moon. Behind us
history. Repeating herself
with lips of past Lovers. Tears
she fed me. I drunk
from her forbidden well. With drapes
drawn. For the world to see
she presented sentiments. For another,
we created passion from pain. As I rocked
her to slumber. It was Poetry
the way I remembered. Her to be
full of sorrow and suffering. These feelings
I longed for. Her heart
I desired to capture. In spite
of pride. I should have
discovered and left. Her
I love. Eternally

Strain

The past is not a place to go
Only weeds of reminders breed
Past pain
A lesson unlearned
Melodies of memories
Of how it aches
Strong hands
Parts that don't fit
The heaviness of emptiness
That's how it feels back there
Disregarded
Discarded
Trash
Reaping of history
I have revisited
My reflection
Stained in temporary glass
Broken twice
Between curiosity
And a need
To know
Why
It hurts
So damn good

A Purge

Fingers down throat
Searching a way
To bring up my mistakes
A lack of control
To control the lack
I'm broken in the middle
Sewed up
A wounded womb
Barren of everything
Aside secrets
Behind white doors
Four walls
No windows
Just me
The heaving
And my Blue God

Dear Audre,

I wish I were more like you...brave and willing to take on the challenges of this world. I wish that fear was something that I knew nothing about and that I could move freely without the weight of life holding me down. I want to breathe without permission and leave this hell of a place. Everyone is so fucking negative and our lives are what we have made them, I want freedom from responsibility and I don't really give a damn about your love life or mine...your ungrateful kin or mine...I just want to fly away from this moment into a space just for me, a rest near water...a spring to drink from without worry, need, or regret. I want to hear my voice and not all these others...I want silence to discover once again a way out of here. I want to flee her and her and all the things that are grossly heavy in my life...I want to dream a way to paradise. Audre...find me...breathe me, give me some of you to make a path through this nightmare.

In the beginning...I believed in everything and everyone. Today...I believe in nothing but truth.

Life is a lesson in limitations. It has a way of humbling you daily. I am so lopsided after bearing the weight of it all, the weight of reality. It is like a wild storm that sneaks up beside you on a sunny day. So unexpected and commanding, beating my heart black and blue.

I was once told..."I believe in lies if they sound good." She was a poet...a real one. Took my soul on a journey of make-believe. Make-believe I am so in love with you, make-believe I trust you and can't breathe without you. Make-believe...we will be forever. Believe in forever...right before my insecurity destroys you.

My heart beats black and blue. Black for torture and blue for water. Silent tears are never heard, they are masked as control. My heart beats black and blue, worn and ragged. My heart beats for you...even when you have bathed my existence away.

I swim to get away from you...from me...from us. I swim to forget the pain, to silence the noise, to reach GOD. I swim to erase it, if only for a second...I swim.

In the beginning...there were words. In the end...silence.

~The Commencement

Relief

Today I cried
Don't know why
I just did

It was weighty
That something
Faceless
Anonymous
Shame
On me

I gave in
To the well in my throat
Pushed self beside
A closed corner
Curved over
Like a ball
In a pitcher's hand
I drowned

Today I took a shower
In my own pain
And died

Double-Dealing

If you had sat still
With an uncluttered heart
My offering would have come
As easy as my voice
Could have been remembered

In the feet of your mind
A place where no other woman
Could walk nor sign my name

If you had been responsive
You would have known
Just how angry silence can be

How the red dress worn to bed
Was only a flag
Colored in acknowledgment
Of my pain

You not knowing the difference
Between our tracks and taste
Was alarming enough

Did she remind you just that much of me
Or was it fear
That kept you from owning up
To your shit

And yes...it reeked
But...we all have flaws
One of yours
Is not having ears
Nor the courage
To confess it

Sincerely -Your Fool

Not another night of you
Sitting on my soul like this

Just leave
Save me this mess
I have settled into
Looking like a fool

Pondering everything
I can remember of you
How deep you dug
Into my heart
Just to slay me
Into this fool I am

Dreaming up ways
And days
Til I hold you again

I am this fool
Still searching of ways
To bump into you

To rid myself
Of picking up the pieces
And trying to live with
This hole

Right dead in the center
Of my world
Is you

Me...this fool
I am for you

Bad Habit

I could make love to you
A gazillion times
Would be like the first time

You said my name
As you exhaled
My smoke
I grasped

Your scent
Was peppermint on an autumn day

I shall never forget
How it poured
Confusion on my heart

Turned into remains of your fire
My mind
Stalked by memories

Your love
Is terminal

Never Love

It was only a need to be loved
Not that we were in love

The way that our mouths opened
Without trust
Was just a mutual dedication

When we longed for the real thing
Anything was healthier than empty

She filled me up
As I occupied her

We loved
In spite of our hearts
We felt like anybody
Who was needed by somebody

I loved her
She loved me
When love was something that we both desired
More than anything else

We wanted to be loved
So we made love
Without love

She whispered it as I slept
I dispatched it as she worked

We stumbled over it together
Until it sounded right

No, we were not in love

Traces of Her

But we said it
Because it felt good at night
And the thought of being loved
Was astounding
I loved on her
She loved on me
Even if we weren't in love
It was better than
Nothing at all

There comes a time when you have to release those things buried in your soul. Those are the tears that silently crawl from your midsection, to the back of your throat begging to be released. A feeling of misery... that you have nursed to death in your own private hell.

 I move to embrace freedom before slamming the door and pausing between walls that know me intimately. Years incomplete and still counting loudly.

Lord I have regrets and my noose is too tight to fit any more. Sometimes I just want to let go... find a river and make my bed of roses. But I am here... stuck between some bullshit and a wish over candles unlit.

~Fire Starter

Second Time Around

What shall we make of us this round
My love

Is it possible to make our beds and start anew
Patch broken hearts and mend spirits
That are capable of giving absolutely

Love is infinite
So I have heard

Just when I thought I had beheld your depths
You became bottomless

I'm focused on dying
This round
No maybe
Or perhaps

I'm willing
To do whatever it takes
To live our forever

Get off this dead-ended road
Leading to nowhere

But here
I am waiting
For you
On us
To penetrate our love
In this wide open space

Unkindled

Try wrapping your arms
Around a new idea
To discover a barren heart
Dependent on old flames to burn

She said to stop carrying my past
On curved shoulders
Broken from digging
Graves of past love
Lovers exhausted, aloof
On loving me, ever again

I am waging this war alone
Betting my life away
The way she left me
Unwilling to breathe, getting by on lies

I force feed self daily
To ignore
A filthy spirit
Sitting sucking
On ghost whispering
Saddest truths
As I smolder
Inside a famished shell
Alone

I gave her my heart,
The last thing I own
I gave it all
For her word
To love
Not wound
Like this

We come like a burst of air with a clean slate...we leave as nothing more than unsettled dust. Time is the one regret that cannot be converted.

I am in a place of travel. A place where your life begins to dance in front of you, only the steps are too fast to mimic. You can only watch what has been, what is, and what is to become.

Nostalgic

Suppose I love
Lying here picking apart scabs
Just to relive you

Those biting and sugar laced moments
Of you

Suppose I like dying repeatedly
Needing to experience how
A heart can stop beating
Mid a goodbye
I did not see coming
Even the way you left
Was a surprise

I always thought it would be over
One of our coffins
Tears watering the roses
Of yesterday
Not you handing back my heart
With a rushed
Two syllable word
Minus an apology

Was I ever worthy to you
Worth an 'I love you'
And 'if you need me, just call'

You left so quickly
In the dusk of a morning
Born to soon
Was our death

Just a part of what I have to go through

Traces of Her

On this journey

A mere pause in my path
That has left me tugging
At this pain

I constantly borrow
From the day you abandoned me
Crowning me an orphan of love

And if you ever wonder...
I'm still here
Same chair
Same position
Same expression
You buried me in

You said it was because of me that you no longer bless the world with your voice. You blamed it all on me...took your verses and swallowed them, refusing to share that GOD giving gift. You knew just how I felt and what I would give just to read you again. But there is nothing left but this animated silence from you. You torture me...even today. And every woman since has brought your pain to me. Cheating when I didn't, lying when I can't...leaving me again. Maybe it's a curse...love that is.

Did your pen really die, or is it in a box beneath that hot heart? You were never you...just some stranger to my world trying to live a fairytale by night. When the sun finally stood up again...you were quick to undress and pile your face full of mystery. I look to you and I don't see you, a ghost in your smile, a phantom with your breast, a nightmare with your smell. Why did you leave me here? I too can adjust to change. I too believe in choosing a different path when the current one no longer fits. I would take you naked eyes or underlined...even when I say no. I was just desperately trying to hold on to some sort of dignity that doesn't make any sense now that you are gone. How do I forget you...let go of a distant past...or tell me how to find you again.

Hopefully you will come across my words and revive your pen. Maybe you will write of me still...good or poor.

Am I really the reason for the death of your pen...or are you hiding from me. I only want your words...everything else I already own.

~Death of Her Pen

After Birth

Just like that
You left
My heart bursting

Wondering when
I will be able to release you

And
If tomorrow ever opens
Will my winter end
Or snow me under
Because
I dared to love you

Am I forgettable
As the love we made
On the floor

My devotion
Is still attached
To those scars on my knees
From promises made
By you woman

I am not ashamed
Still here settled
On notes you wrote me

They were your words
You slid down my throat
From the tip of your tongue
You made a noose
For me to swing

Now allow me to die
Swallow those lies
So that I may drown
In your midsection
And stretch out all this pain
That you might feel
My Love
And birth me again

A Woman's Worth

This woman, she is a mystery
Her crying eyes and her stuffed heart
I marvel over her day after day.

This woman, I wonder what matters to her
She adjusts with the direction of the wind
I want to know what makes a difference in her world

This woman is appealing in all of her emotions
She pretends to fix easy
But I see her bond...undone effortlessly

This woman changes with the sun...so sweet beneath the moon
There is something I want from this woman
But I question my own reasons, her pain is beckoning me
I want to quiet her aches...eavesdrop on her wisdom

This woman said she would make a great phone friend
As I lie here wanting more of this woman
She simply adjusts

She...

She leaves easy...as soon as I step away she falls into the night. Like wind she becomes when I come undone. Her love lies and stays gone overnight sometimes. I wonder where she goes when I'm left alone. She leaves easy when I let go...a storm she becomes with her rain in my eyes. When she returns I wonder what she left behind, how much love I have lost...what condition her heart in. She loves me without ends...she loves me just as much as she hates me. I can't blame her...I despise me most of the time...but she's my teacher.

She likes to play the radio...my favorite song at times. She likes to play with heartstrings...especially mine. She likes to play innocent when I'm not interested...she likes to play with me. She loves me and I love her...maybe that should be enough. But times are challenging and this is not a test, just my heart wide open and disobedient. I'm not perfect...just the best at love, because I get it. I'm just waiting on her to recognize that I am a gift...giving it freely without charge. She likes to play with her words, choose the right things to say. I like to read between lines and I always hear what is not said. Maybe we are a perfect match.

Emaciated Honey

We spin it
Hoping for wings
Wanting to fly
Far from creation
It is biting lies
That we swallow
In the end
Inflamed bellies
Full of dreams
We lace
Traps
To settle in
Believing
That She catches
My whispers
Burnt beneath tongue
I am wasting
Breathing
Away
What suffers here
My love
Is demanding
Swarming butterflies
Midsection this magic
I melt away
To embrace
Rose painted moments
When she provided me
Air

Skeletal Remains

Draw a line
To the end
Of us
Show me where
It begins
To rain our song

Sketch the reasons
In stone
Please
Do not leave
Anything rare

Display me your future
A shield for my today

How long will you love me?
Is not a query
Just heart pondering
Engravings for headstones

There comes a time for everyone and everything...today is a time for tears. Today is a time for soul cleansing for letting go and holding on. Today is all about the sanity and lunacy of it all. Today is about standing in the rain and enjoying the aches. Today is about getting out of line, out of positions and situations that are too tight and too small to live in. Today is about home runs and avoiding having to hit all the bases. Today is about her and realizing that I am simply a bird with no destination...

~Flying in the Rain

Just Listen

Waves are for swimming
Why am I going under
Here is my hand
I keep offering
Over your head

Do you hear me now
When I shout so loud
Does it vibrate understanding
Or am I still
Your dried up mold

Do not speak so quickly
Listen to this heart of mine
It beats reality

Will you sing my lyrics
The way I harmonized
Or bleed out the center

I am crawling to you
Lend me your time

Insecure

A certain fire
Dissolving into ice
My love
For you
It hurts
When you abandon
My heart
With your insecurities
You bleed me
Dry
Are my eyes
Only for you

Considering

I think. . .
I choose mistakes over exact
Ache over love
It feels right.

I think. . .
I'd rather mislay than to triumph
Nothing to search through
I get bored with affection

I think. . .
We truly get what we deserve
What we strive for

But what about the boundless
No hope
Little faith
Always hungry

What happens to us?
Hands packed
Arms still reaching for fulfillment

I think. . .
For the restless
There is no conclusion…
Just greed.

Faded Pictures

We sit on the same bench
Opposite our hearts
Where I have curved her into a stranger

She says
My name is no longer a melody that draws her near

And
We are not lovers like we pretend to be

As natives question our relations
She bows in silence
I smile and nod alone

She is still afraid of what she knows
I have long gone without her knowledge

Soon
She will attempt to open her eyes
A lot too late
To kiss me my perfect lips
Attached to another

Audre,

I missed you this weekend, she is jealous of the time spent with you. The way I desired to finger your hand in the theater as we sat silenced in our own shame, her more than I. I knew you would not take notice of the roaming eyes. You would have glanced my way several times and I yours. There would have been private forays of bodies in the darkness and lips crossing paths. Not awkward stillness cloaking us like a grave. I wish you would have been here to conclude the movie with me, this need is reckoning, you are haunting and all I lack is your presence. You are the weakness in me that I shall forever possess.

Me-

Traces of Her

www.ingramcontent.com/pod-product-compliance
Lightning Source LLC
Chambersburg PA
CBHW071416040426
42444CB00009B/2269